But this morning,
I found a lighter heart.

Poems from the Pond

Second Edition, 2015

Edited by Laurie David

Permission to republish all poems and excerpts from *Growing Up in Old Age*
provided by Margaret Howe Freydberg

Cover Photo by Eli Dagostino

Endliner photo by Yann Meersseman

Permission to publish "A query to Richard Reston" and republish
"Peggy Freydberg, Who Dwells in the Present" provided by the Vineyard Gazette

Permission to republish photos previously featured in the Vineyard Gazette
provided by the Vineyard Gazette and Mark Lovewell

Permission to publish "On the Occasion of Peggy's 100th Birthday"
provided by John Maloney

Book design and production by April Lizardo
and Integrated Communications Los Angeles, ICLA

ISBN 978-0-692-37653-9

Hybrid Nation
11812 San Vicente Blvd., 4th Floor | Los Angeles, California 90049

Poems from the Pond

107 Years of Words and Wisdom
The Writings of Peggy Freydberg

Edited by Laurie David

"With an unflinching eye and a compassionate heart, Peggy Freydberg has looked deeply into what it means to live a long life. In pulse-quickening poems of stunning insight and artistry, she probes the necessity of loss and the exhilarations of love."

Geraldine Brooks
Pulitzer Prize-winning novelist

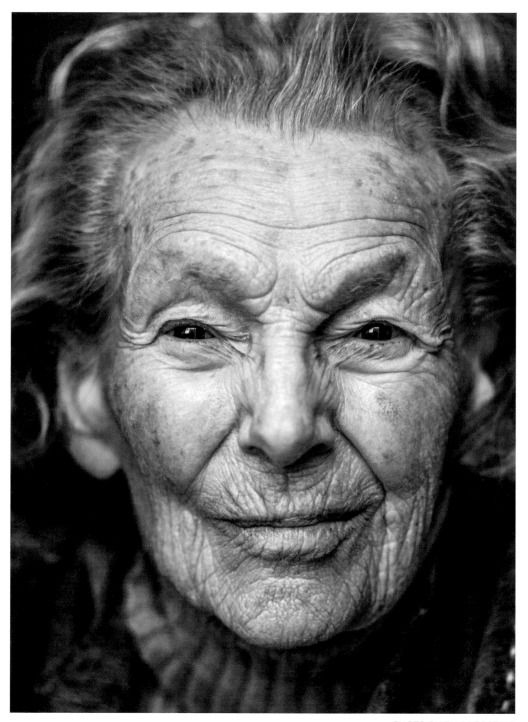

Contents

Foreword

I first met Peggy Freydberg in 1994 at a women's symposium on Martha's Vineyard. I run a writers' workshop in Chilmark and was asked to speak about storytelling. Peggy was a novelist turned poet and was invited to recite some of her poems. I was nervous. I had just moved to the Island year round and didn't know what the winter community would be like. Peggy was older than me and since I am always on the lookout for mentors and teachers, she seemed like a perfect candidate, maybe even a potential new friend.

And then she stood up and read her poem "A Letter to My Family, Explaining How I Feel about My Cats" and I fell madly in love with her. The poem had humor and passion and a wisdom that told me she wasn't just older than me: she was way wiser. And I wanted to be near it.

But then life got in the way and despite the fact that we lived one mile apart, it took another twenty-one years for us to reconnect.

The impetus for that began in the summer of 2014 when I wrote a piece for NPR about not paying attention to my intuition. I had three dear friends, whose faces had come clearly into my head, when a little voice whispered "call them," but I did nothing about it. And then one by one, within ten days of each other, I learned that all three had died. It was a serious wake-up call. Learning curves being what they are, I made a promise to myself that when I thought about someone in that I-should-call-them way, then that's what I was going to do.

So a few days later, when out of nowhere Peggy popped into my mind, I quickly got on the phone and dialed. "I have a poet friend visiting me. Can we come over and see you?" She couldn't have said yes faster. We made our plan and that's how this belated, delayed friendship interruptus began again.

As we entered her living room I realized I had forgotten how elegant and beautiful she was. Awestruck, I asked her if she would read a few of her poems to my friend. She declined, saying she had macular degeneration and couldn't see to read anymore.

And so, we read to her... her work, from her books. After about four poems I was so blown away by the power of the words, I said "Peggy, how come you're not famous???" And she responded humbly "I don't know."

Immediately, I mean at once, I knew exactly what I was going to do: organize a local celebration of Peggy and her poems.

On my Facebook page (which I am really working on trying to visit now and then) I wrote an invitation for friends to come to my small studio and hear some brilliant poetry written by a local treasure but read to her and us, by others.

I rented chairs. I called the Vineyard Gazette and the MV Times. I called the local cable station to record it and I made a little stage with two seats and a table between them. Just stargazer lilies, a candle, Peggy in one chair and the reader next to her, set the scene.

For the next hour I saw that it wasn't just a schoolgirl crush. Peggy's words moved everyone, cut every one right to the gut, were accessible, were readable, were musical. You could have heard a pin drop in that room. People were listening with every cell of their beings. They were crying, they were sighing, and they were recognizing themselves and their own experiences.

She's a storyteller, that woman. A truth teller. She writes symphonies in words. At the end of the readings there was a spontaneous standing ovation. And I saw Peggy's face: radiant!

After the last guest had left and we were decompressing, Peggy said to me, "I have wondered why I have lived to be this old and now I know why: it was to experience this day." I cried (for the fourth time that afternoon). My husband lifted her into her wheelchair and guided her to the waiting car. A friend drove her the five minutes back to her home on Stonewall Pond.

This is a beautiful story but I still haven't told you the best part. Peggy didn't even start writing poetry until she had turned 90. And here is the kicker: at the time of our reading, she was 106!

The aftermath of that special afternoon continues to reverberate. Poetry brought Peggy and me together and now another new

PEGGY AND NANCY AFTER THE POETRY READING
PHOTO COURTESY OF LYNN CHRISTOFFERS

friend: Laurie David. Laurie knew someone who was coming to the reading and got a third-hand invitation to attend, which she did. She was so moved by the afternoon she lingered long after everyone else had left and secured one of the few books Peggy, in her shaky hand, was able to sign that day.

The next day Laurie emailed me, "I can't stop thinking about that gorgeous poetry and the inspiring 106-year-old woman who wrote it."

She wanted to come with me on my next visit (and many more after that). It didn't take long for Laurie to propose the idea for this book you now hold in your hands. "We have an obligation to share these poems with everyone," she said excitedly.

We think Poems from the Pond is a fitting tribute to the power of this unique poet's gift and an inspiration for anyone and everyone who is wading through life's mysteries.

Peggy is our own personal Poet Laureate and we want to share her with the world. She is proof that creativity has no age limit and that words on the page are like salve for the heart.

She writes about love, death, food, friends, wine, loss, aging, and of course, cats. You'll find yourself weeping and smiling and wishing you could live right next door so you could see… the hymn of the setting sun… or… the old stone wall to keep the sheep from wandering…

In the middle of one of our favorites, she says:

I am bare now
Cool to the fire of sunsets
Gladly undressed of them

I have done with my
monogrammed vision
I would rather in my old age
look at the center of a flower,
or watch the ancient dance
of a cat whirling up
to catch a butterfly.

Laurie and I welcome you into Peggy's rich Vineyard life. We welcome you to her Stonewall Pond and all the sunrises, sunsets, kayaks, birds, and lovers she has watched her many, many years from the living room window. If you possibly can, come in spring…

So you can see the boisterous splash of forsythia
which cannot wait to get here first
and shout about it

Nancy Aronie

top: STONE WALL POND / bottom: PEGGY'S HOME
PHOTOS BY ELI DAGOSTINO

PHOTO COURTESY OF THE VINEYARD GAZETTE AND MARK LOVEWELL

POEMS

CHORUS OF CELLS

Every morning,
even being very old,
(or perhaps because of it),
I like to make my bed.
In fact, the starting of each day
unhelplessly,
is the biggest thing I ever do.
I smooth away the dreams disclosed by tangled sheets,
I smack the dented pillow's revelations to oblivion,
I finish with the pattern of the spread exactly centered.
The night is won.
And now the day can open.

All this I like to do,
mastering the making of my bed
with hands that trust beginnings.
All this I need to do,
directed by the silent message
of the luxury of my breathing.

And every night,
I like to fold the covers back,
and get in bed,
and live the dark, wise poetry of the night's dreaming,
dreading the extend of its improbabilities,
but surrendering to the truth it knows and I do not;
even though its technicolor cruelties,
or the music of its myths,
feels like someone else's experience,
not mine.

I know that I could no more cease
to want to make my bed each morning,
and fold the covers back at night,
than I could cease
to want to put one foot before the other.

Being very old and so because of it,
all this I am compelled to do,
day after day,
night after night,
directed by the silent message
of the constancy of my breathing,
that bears the news I am alive.

What is so wrong?
So much of what I've wanted,
once gotten,
has been replaced
by other wantings.
And thus no wanting
has ever been a final getting.

Slight fame seemed as insubstantial as
a spider's web
that can be demolished
by any hand with purpose.

The blossoming of my mind,
so long unfertilized,
I found to be a great substantiality,
but still no answer
to what it could not cease
from searching for.

The light within,
of love
still leaves a great illumined place that seems,
like space,
infinity that has no answering.

Not even the discovery
of my self —
that be-all, end-all
of sophisticated wanting —
has ever satisfied my longing
for some unimagined transformation,
opening to boundless ways of being
yet unfound.

What is so wrong?
Why is it that the more I get,
the more I want?
And that no getting satisfies,
but is, instead, surrounded with a nimbus of bright gold,
to glorify disappointment?

. . . . .

But think.
Stand up
and walk away from
calling wanting wrong.
Don't pummel solid rock
with helpless fists.
Let the rock be.

Find the part of wanting
that is every person's recognition
of the endless possibilities of himself.
We shape the world towards joy,
with our dreams of it.

Find the part of wanting
that is hoping —
even for consciousness yet unfound —
and dare to give it praise.

The title is from a poem by Walt Whitman, in Leaves of Grass.

MORNINGS AT SEVEN

Wild geese stir in the early morning calm
with the ripple of their wake.
Far off,
near the shore's arm of dune that holds the pond,
a kayak glides,
someone seeking peace
and looking up to find it in the sky.

A sudden commotion of the water at my shore!
Two swimmers diving in together
side by side exactly.
Man and woman —
I can see the sickle-splash of arms and legs in ardent crawl,
and the watery tumult of pumping feet.

But more, and
unmistakable,
is a joyous energy of purpose in the two of them,
heading out.
And a determination to be swimming side by side,
exactly;
so that in coming up for air, their eyes can meet.

The seriousness of their purpose shouts to heaven,
and gives this pond and sky
a grounding and a glory,
announcing that their heading out, together, side by side,
is no more the single purpose of their beings,
than is the night of sleeping side by side.

And they have found that that's the simple whole of it.

The title is from the poem "Pippa's Song," by Robert Browning.

GETTING THERE

Do you ever pause,
in the midst of the effort
of trying to be known —
which suddenly strikes you as
too much and
too hard and
too perpetual —
to consider loosening the muscles at the back of your neck,
and looking up to find the sky?

This I did,
yesterday.
I was driving home from a gallery opening
of an artist's work I knew,
at which I had said to everyone I met,
fortissimo,
having rehearsed the line before I got there:
"Her work is both exact and infinite,"
holding in one hand a plastic glass of harsh white wine,
and with the other,
groping for my pearls
whose warmth from being round my neck,
is me,
is memory of shame,
is grounding,
and a reminder of what I know
about the loose content
of being plainspoken.

At the State Forest,
a flock of wild turkeys
emerging from between the trees to cross the road,
brought traffic to a halt.

With tiny-headed, brainless hauteur,
strutting,
stepping exactly,
taking their time,
black and stately —
like tenured professors in swinging robes
sway slowly in a line at graduation —
they headed for the other side,
a few stopping midway to consider
in fussy deliberation,
a few scuttling back to where they'd come from,
only one or two getting it right the first time,
the rest getting it right,
finally.

The cars in the other lane start up,
ready to move on.
But I do not.
Under the heavy trees at dusk,
holding my pearls,
I wait in the great silence of my watchfulness,
until the last wild turkey,
following the others,
has crossed the road
to safety.

MAKING SURE

There it is —
That little instrument of deception —
a light-weight metal comb with squiggly prongs,
no bigger than two postage stamps placed side by side,
Resting in an antique Luster teacup
on the bathroom counter in a path of sun.

The miracle of this ordinary little comb
is that,
invisibly,
it holds my labored coif in place,
as no barrette, or hair pins, or hair net
ever has.
Or ever will. (*The stores no longer have it. Discontinued, I am told.)

I need this little comb.
I could almost say —
I love this tending little comb.
I never pick it up to fix it in my hair,
without a sense of being ready
to go forward.

One day,
In a roaring gale from off the sea,
my heavy hair spilled down,
sent flying — hair net, hair pins, little comb.
In lashing strands,
it whipped across my face — into my eyes, my mouth.
Wonderful wildness!
For a second, I was in a place I'd never been before.

     The wind died down,
     And so did I.
     My little comb was gone.

. . . . .

Two years have passed.
And every time I walk along the driveway of the Tisbury Printer,
(where I always thought I must have lost the comb),
I look down with hope that never loses freshness,
thinking I will see it — rusted now,
down in the deep, green grass.

The search goes on.
I cannot keep myself from searching.
Although I have,
at last,
begun to wonder
just what it is I'm looking for.

PHOTO COURTESY OF THE VINEYARD GAZETTE AND MARK LOVEWELL

OF TWO MINDS

Yesterday I was heavy-hearted.
And everywhere I looked
I saw the melancholy winter eyes of the very old,
superimposed on the smudge of the maples' red budding,
on the pale green mist of the wild cherry's leafing,
on the boisterous yellow splash of the forsythia,
which cannot wait to get here first, and shout about it.

In the orange cups of the white narcissus,
or amidst the beach plum's branches, blistered with tight buds,
I saw a thousand excommunicated eyes,
watching what's been given birth again,
watching the earth,
and not themselves,
come back to life.

But this morning,
I found a lighter heart.
I bent to pick a stalk of fragrant bells
from the lily of the valley's tiny jade green forest,
and to pull the cold green watercress from the cold swift brook.
And everywhere I looked,
The unbelonging eyes were gone.

BOOK SIGNING

All my life,
I have wanted to be shown respect
for a mind not apparent to anyone,
not even, at first,
to myself.
So there was never any respect
of the kind I craved,
shown to me.

It has always been a raging indignity
to be incapable of thought,
and to be known for that;
to be to all appearances
childishly emotional,
while knowing, somehow,
that I was more than that.
Though really I don't wonder.
For what the others heard,
I realize now,
Were only disconnected stores of second-hand utterances,
and spumes of social babble,
like a child's entreaty
to be heard, as well as seen.

But gradually,
and it was a long and disbelieving process,
I found the source of my capability.

Revealed at last,
protesting with frantic hope
its long neglect,
not fetal now, but
out from its dark drowning,
my mind began to rage for its rightful use.
Even in the flouncing
of my emotion's can-can competition,
my mind had grown too demanding,
and too intentional,
to be ignored.

I began to live in a new place.
I loved it there,
wading through the
long, think grasses of words,
pastures of ideas,
where I had never been before.
I loved the grace and fury
of this place arrived at,
where I was destined to live,
and from then on,
did.
And where the language of my mind's unfolding,
became a book.

But then,
and I must say,
like the relentless beating of a small hammer,
my mind,
raging for its rightful use,
demanded,
finally,
its rightful recognition.
It had been too long buried,
not to need,
with its deliverance,
the recognition
of those who had been sure
of its non-existence.

"I never knew you could think like that."
The most treasured words of my life.
Though he had had no way of knowing
about a mind that raged in darkness
for his approval of it.

But his,
anyone's approval of my mind,
has no lasting power.
And so remind me of yesterday,
when I was held from noon to night
within the strong embrace of an approval
I felt sure would never let me go.
When I stood on a platform,
microphone-armoured,
and as I looked at the faces in the audience,
and even before I began to talk,
I felt, in one miraculous contraction
of the scattered zones of self,
that I was justly there,
and that, as fully as I have ever known belief,
I believed those words of mine
I was about to speak.

There I was, then, yesterday,
transcending person
in the justness of belief.
Feeling neither more nor less,
but like a space between two points,
all of a sudden immense in my capability,
expanding like rising dough out to my edges.
Or, like a full chord of myself,
in tune and orchestrated and crescendo-ed.
For one rare moment I was fully furnished
with my capability.

Perhaps an uncloaking
of the complete extent of capability
can feel immense to anyone.
There is an immensity in completion,
in a power once ungathered,
now gathered
and made manifest.
I was feeling a power without limits
in the blossoming of what I was able to be.
I would never have to worry about another thing
in my whole life,
if I could always feel this immaculate puissance.

Then tell me why,
during the night of that day's confidence,
I was gradually without it?
Why, as I lay thinking in the dark,
I allowed the whole and sure platform
of my capability
to collapse?
Did I really sell "almost all of my books,"
as I so proudly announced to him
when I got home —
I had been too giddy
as I signed them,
to count;
enough to verify my longing claims?
Were my boasts facts?
And if not,
would I be obliged
to discontinue boasting?

After hours of lying sleepless in the dark,
reduced to all the pieces
of the discord of myself,
suddenly I lay still,
re-living the immensity
of a pure point reached,
returned,
that easily,
to capability,
enjoying its companionship.

How infirm is my belief
in the speaker of the speech.
How immediately indefensible
my capability becomes,
with the slightest questioning of it.
So tell me about yesterday.
And tell me what it is in me
that does not need to boast,
yet must continue in the disharmony
of blowing myself up
into the wrong immensity?

THE FINAL CHANGE

Being blind,
the fundamental thing my sister could not tolerate,
was change.
If her panic-fluttering fingers,
groping ahead in apprehensive search
for the familiar,
touched something alien,
she would halt, freeze, and then begin to whimper softly,
in heaven knows what depths of terror.

    The years went by.
    Her innocent, heroic heart gave out at last.
    She died.
    And I grew old.

In the course of time,
one night in sudden darkness of a blackout,
I lived my sister's panic
while groping for the light switch on the wall
I knew was there but could not find.
And, with the loss of some essential faith
in what is naturally due me,
like the permanence of my breathing,
all at once my blind eyes saw my death,
as fear-ful as the thousand deaths my sister died
each time she touched the empty dark.

HOLDING MACALISTAIR

I am sitting in the thick light of sunset
slanting through the embrasured window
of a small room
at the top of the lighthouse,
high above the cliffs.

Over me —
in the glassed-in dome of this red brick tower
I have circularly and slowly climbed —
is the mighty light,
flashing its search far out across
the certain calm and rage of seas.
And,
in my arms I hold Macalistair,
my great-grandson,
who is two and a half months old,
left alone with me for the first time,
even held by me for the first time.

Outside, on a narrow circling balcony
so thinly railed
that only migrating Monarch butterflies seem safe there,
my granddaughter and her husband stand,
unsure,
stirred,
looking at the sea,
looking at the rocks below the cliffs.

The importance of holding Macalistair
hits me right away.
I have begun to talk softly and continuously to him,
finding myself in a place I've never been;
and awed by how heavy —
like a life-size marble cupid —
this tiny weight of a baby is,
as though he were packed solid
with the whopping energy it takes
to know what's going on
that never has gone on before,
and must be held within the casing of his skin
to fuel concentration on this newness
that has his mother's face,
and yet,
bewilderingly,
does not;
and on a voice that woos,
that penetrates to where his smile comes from —
the kind of sound he knows he's heard before,
but this time,
can't be certain of.

How still he is,
concentrating,
mobilizing.
Some babies jab their tiny arms,
and romp their tiny legs,
with the important bustle of experiencing.
Not Macalistair.
His experiencing —
though he is fit to bursting with it —
is at this moment,
motionless.
His spellbound eyes,
taking me in,
are steady as two stars.

Held fast,
our looking is.
He searching.
I searching.
He discovering.
I discovering him
discovering.

My awe has turned to radiance,
the kind the cells feel.

FALLING IN LOVE

What kind of an instrument was I,
when he found it,
and, because his blood impelled him to,
daringly, for caution was very strong,
reached a broad, square finger
and plucked for the first time,
one if its strings?

I could have called myself a Stradivarius,
for though I, of course, was just an ordinary violin,
waiting,
ready to be held for the first time in a musician's hands,
primed to be played,
mobilized by all my busy genes
to become music —
when first I felt the quiver
of its stirring sound,
I became, imparadised,
the most priceless stringed instrument
on the face of the earth.

After all those years
of lying in the curvaceous coffin of a velvet-lined violin case
snapped shut,
unborn, but
fully contoured waiting to emerge
and breathe to make my destined music —
one day he came
and dared to pluck a string.

Life made its first whole sound.

CALL ME BUT LOVE AND I'LL
BE NEW BAPTIZED

I stood in the doorway of my dining room,
beside the man I was falling in love with.
We had been drinking lots of wine by candlelight and firelight,
talking about being already more than half-way through
our half-filled lives.
and we were now unharnessed.
I was saying things I'd never known I knew.
My mind's time had stopped.
And with slow dazzle,
my heart's timelessness
may have begun.

As we stood,
Richard Strauss's Der Rosenkavalier
which had been playing quietly in the living room —
solitary, far from our mood,
softening corners —
burst astonishingly into the great crescendo of the waltz.

I turned to look at him.
Grave, startled,
he looked back at me.
And this had meaning.
It had connection with the sudden blast of music
which was rising up in me like an eruption
of the earth beneath my feet.

Then all at once,
instead of body,
I was fountain.
I was not woman,
I was water with another name.
With perfect, innate delirium,
I was a torrent
sparkling from the earth
up to the sky.

The earth had quaked,
and blown me straight up.
And, I could feel that he was quivering on a launch pad,
that we were racing up and up together,
that we were an air-borne couple,
bombing upwards
towards a heaven's surprise.

With each fusillade of music,
I stabbed my arms towards heaven's great, waiting emptiness,
feeling that each ascending lunge
of fountain-music jetting from my finger-tips
was draining out of me the sludge of long-unloving blood;
while in its place,
transfused clean blood hosed upwards
towards a prophecy of re-creation.

And I was on my way to it.
At last.
Believing in my arrival,
straining with every fiber of my being,
I rose,
and kept on rising.

The title is from William Shakespeare's Romeo and Juliet.

WHAT I ALWAYS WANTED TO BE IS BARE

I am sitting on the steps of a small, empty old farm house,
under a lilac bush as high as the roof.

You are sitting against a tree a few feet away.

Here is an essential bareness,
a small entirely empty house —
two rooms,
a lilac bush,
a hill sloping down from the front stoop
to the valley.

Be with me in this bareness.
We need to be what we are —
two empty rooms of an old house and a lilac bush —
your lost bareness,
and mine

Fear of bareness bought the Ferrari in the three car garage of
the house we built thirty years ago
with Fortuny draperies hanging along the
pitted lavender window panes bought at auction
and installed in the dining room
paneled with dark wood found in an old house in Connecticut.

Fear of bareness bought the Ferrari
and the Fortuny draperies
and the wines of the right year.

What covers our souls is the silk wallpaper.
What keeps us strangers is what we think we need.
When what we need is only the bareness of ourselves.
Only two ancient rooms grateful for being empty,
and an ancient lilac bush giving out sweetness.

I have always wanted to say only three words to you:
You. Me. Us.
No one of them adjectived beyond its essentiality.
Only you, and me, and us,
bare as the day we were born.
I have always wanted us, bare
on a composted forest floor —
the essential bed.

I sit on the stoop, for a moment knowing bareness absolutely.
You sit against a tree, looking away
toward the valley, planning how much
you will offer Taggert for the house.
There is a part of you that wants
to buy its bareness.

I always wanted, more than silk wallpaper,
bareness.
And I have lived all my life covered up
and trying to be bare.
I have lived all the years of my life with you,
wanting you to be bare,
so that I could be.

Maybe bareness is not what you needed from me.
Maybe you needed the smooth neck that warmed
the string of sixty pearls you gave me for my
sixtieth birthday?
And when the smoothness began to sink into folds,
you were no longer glad for pearls,
for I was now bare
and could not be adorned?

Bareness — beneath the young skin and beneath
the old skin —
did you ever want either?

I mean, did you ever want me?
Or only me, covered?
Because to want me bare,
you would have to be bare.

But I have gotten to need
to be covered.
And so have you.
Our ancient bareness,
yours and mine,
is a communion that can never be.

The world nearly always covers bareness.

THE SWIMMING LESSON

"There's the little family," I cried.
He came to stand beside me,
watching
the splendid slow progress on the pond,
this calm clear summer morning,
of a flotilla of wild geese —
the goose, the gander, and their seven goslings.

Propelled invisibly by busy feet beneath the surface of the water,
they seem as stationary, and as one-dimensional
as a toy of wooden birds strung on a knotted cord.
One only knows they move
because behind the line of them,
A V-shaped wake appears,
and slowly widens.

We stand,
this man and I,
so old,
so near our endings,
watching
the miniature and mighty convoy
moving in a line as straight as though a ruler had underscored it —
the great, unerring, long-necked gander leading,
the seven goslings, way below him, following,
each space between obedient baby birds, not by a fraction different,
and bringing up the rear,
in queenly and impeccable positioning,
the goose who hatched and laid
the seven golden eggs,
gliding in serene pride of it.

If I were a gosling, I thought,
I would never have to doubt
my trust in those two parents,
who fly free and wild,
and mate for life,
and who conduct their lives,
and guard their nests,
with a nobility I ascribe to them
because their behavior
is my definition of it.

I have a sudden recognition
of why it is that he, and I, are standing here.
I may have always known,
in languageless recesses of myself,
about the primal and perfected craft
of the guiding,
and the guarding,
of existence.
But today,
with wondrous grasping,
I see,
in a goose, a gander,
and their seven goslings,
a stately demonstration
of First Purpose,
wearing its eternal smile.

We stand together,
he and I,
so old,
so near our endings,
and watch,
with wonder,
and with wanting,
the pure and sure beginnings
of seven goslings
being taught to swim in a straight line.

PHOTO COURTESY OF YANN MEERSSEMAN / VINEYARD COLORS

ALL THE PEOPLE IN THIS PLAY ARE
HERE EXCEPT THE LEADING MAN

You live in a house on a hill that spreads down to the ocean,
the heavy lace of an ancient stone wall marks the beginning
of its descent.
You see the white line of surf,
and hear its sound.
You tell yourself in laughing language, how lucky you are
that you can still hear it,
even though you're growing old.
And you remind yourself how blessed you are to live in such a
spot, in the house you and your husband built together,
with hammer and nails and a power saw.

You have three daughters and a son and nine grandchildren — all,
metaphorical dikes against the rising floodwaters of time and trouble.
They are there, all thirteen of them — joy, consanguinity, self, bulwark,
immortality.
And you have friends, and friends, and friends...
"The trouble is," you say, "I do not have my husband."

At evening, in the northern pasture,
sheep run bleating to be fed,
while you sit in your living room with a friend,
and eat cucumber sandwiches and drink vodka,
exploring your heart.
Your old white cat with one eye
spreads himself warmly and broadly and heavily on your lap,
the consolation of his fur is under your hand.
Your other companion, an old English cocker,
is lying on the window seat next to your chair,
as permanent and as sure
as the old rock wall beyond it, and the sloping pasture and the sea.
He is the part of your heart your husband did not have.
Children, grandchildren, friends, chickens, cats, dogs, owls,
horses — yes, once, briefly, a horse took shelter in your dining room
— all swarm through your house in a mighty tide of life.

You and I are laughing over a book of marvelous, crazy paintings,
one of them a sheep alone on a small raft in a wild, storm-dark sea.
Like you?
Like me?
But you can laugh, you have always laughed,
and always will,
no matter what comes
in the way of storms.

I wonder if you laugh when you're alone.
Perhaps, to keep your spirits up, you do.
Or else you laugh to ridicule the paradox
of seeming to have everything that anyone would want,
while knowing that the thing you want the most,
you do not have.

After you left my house last Sunday night,
you stood for a long time, outside,
looking at the stars,
consulting them,
before getting into your car and driving home
to all the unconnected joys of your life,
that float like lily pads
on unsure depths.

HE LOVES ME, HE LOVES ME NOT

Driving home last night from the party,
I happened to glance at my hand
on the steering wheel,
and saw that it was bare —
no ring.

I did not believe it.
But I did, because of the way it made me feel.
I have felt this way when I have heard of a death
I did not want to believe.

How strange
that I had decided last evening,
with an unheard-of decisiveness,
to wear that ring to the party because
it would match the colors of what I was wearing.
I almost never wear it on the Island
since for this country place it is too lavish —
large round amethyst deep purple as a night sky,
encircled by smaller yellow diamonds
and then a spreading field of white diamond glitter.
Some would call it splurgy
but I would not.
It is too splendid to be splurgy.

There on my finger,
put there without a second's thought,
was that magnificent jewel
selected to be worn
as though by some command.
Obediently,
and with no hesitation,
I had slipped it on my finger
because I was being directed to.

Well, yes, it is/was lavish.
It matters what I call it.
All lavish, costly jewels are conspicuous wealth,
and that, I see, is one of the reasons why this ring matters to me.
"What a gorgeous ring," they say.
I hold my hand off, tilt it toward me,
smile. "Yes. My husband gave it to me."
I am immense
with the affluence of my husband
and his love for me.

This is not to say that the beauty
of my jewel does not give me pleasure.
It does.
I like to look at a beautiful jewel.
But I know it has no deep justness for me
because I understand that the central reason
of my love for it
is because of what it displays.

Why is this loss
such a stabbing
injury?
Why is it so hard to bear?
Is it the loss of
illusion —
the loss of what I wanted to believe
and needed to believe
and have the world believe,
was love?

My engagement ring is another story.
We were young lovers.
On Christmas eve, my lover came to my house
and kneeled to place a small square package
under the tree.
Jessie was there, sipping a martini.
She knew what a small square package
meant.
So did I.
"Open it," she cajoled. "Oh do open it," she begged,
and rolled her treacherous black eyes.
"No," I said, because I knew what was in it.

After Jessie had been tactfully
bade farewell, then, I opened
the small square package.

I'll tell you what my engagement ring
means to me.
First of all, I will describe it:
It is seven moonstones
petaling out like a daisy
from the flower's blue sapphire center.

As I always do with daisies,
I count the petals,
beginning with
"He loves me."
Counted that way,
it always ends that way.

But what woman in love
would begin,
and end with,
"He loves me not?"

In the deepest part of me
which is not a part,
but is the spread of my self's knowing,
I know that the moonstone ring
was pure in your giving,
and pure in my receiving.
It was from your bare heart
to my bare heart.
Young, and in love,
we were both naked, then.

Though did you sense, when you first saw
the moonstone daisy in the jeweler's shop,
when you pondered it,
and when you bought it to give to me,
that you did not then know
whether you loved me, or loved me not?

Did you ever know?

I do not treasure my wedding ring.
In fact, one day I would have none of it,
and took it off for good.

I do not know whether he ever noticed.
He never mentioned it.
Yes, one day, in my imagination,
I threw it into Lake Ontario,
ridding my finger
of its badge of office.
Sometimes I wear it,
but only for the display of having once
been wed.

Now that he is dead, I wear, on my left hand,
where my wedding ring used to be,
the moonstone and turquoise daisy.

Being lovers was the purest.
We should always only have been lovers.

Was it my husband
who commanded me that evening
to wear the ring I later lost?
Let's say, even though I don't believe it, that it was.
Let's say, for instance, that this was
his second giving of that ring to me,
to wear,
but then to lose,
and through the losing of it,
to recover the first,
and truly given ring,
in the little square box,
underneath the Christmas tree.

THE ASSOCIATION OF MAN AND WOMAN

Whatever badness there was,
sometimes
was not of us,
but between us.

Because there was goodness,
which felt like a sure base.
While badness felt only
like incidents upon it.

The badness was only
the way you and I needed to behave,
sometimes.
Not what we were.

The badness was only
a small,
transient,
insignificant
pain,
like the tiny, instant
pain
from the prick of a rose's thorn,
taking joy,
for a second,
away from the fragrance of the rose.

The title is from a poem called "East Coker" by T.S. Eliot in Four Quartets.

REINCARNATION

Come back.
I want you in the other chair,
across from where I sit in mine,
both of us silent,
watching the last log thin to flame-edged coal
above its bed of ashes.

It is the end of the day,
and everything I had to do,
is done.
I have locked the entrance hall front door.
I have filled the cats' blue bowls
with clear, fresh water for the night.
Dinner I have eaten,
automatically,
without remembering to taste it.
Wine,
three glasses of it,
I have tipped into my mouth,
but without the always-hoped-for promise of it.

The night has come,
no difference from the night before,
or from what tomorrow night will be.
It is too early to go bed.
So here I sit,
beside the fading fire,
inert,
empty-handed,
and, empty-minded —
for I have tossed aside,
impatiently,
the book I'm trying to be interested in.

I will not listen to the evening news,
because "news" has to do,
entirely,
with the cruel astonishments of man's existence,
and of all the ways he dies.
And it compounds my frightened aimlessness.
I will not have it!
Whatever beauty
still remains out there,
must be allowed to argue its existence.

. . . . .

Oh, but why list wants, and needs, and lacks,
when what I want and need, and lack the most,
is you in your chair,
I in mine,
sitting by the evening fire,
discovering, for once, the seduction of long silences.

Come back.
We were unfinished.
What did we want and need,
when we sat down at six o'clock,
costumed for courtship —
I had put on pearls

and you had changed your sweater —
and poured our wine with ancient ceremony,
and tried, with words,
to find each other.
Few words we ever said,
were what we could have said,
or even would have said.
The silences we never dared
would have been better
than the subterfuge or courteous, anxious conversation.
Night after night,
year after year,
with passionate, with everlasting expectation,
and with a love that always overrode the way things never
changed,
we kept the pitch of wanting
raging.

. . . . .

Come back.
I want us here,
connected by the peace of new perception,
and by the calm of silence,
languageless,
the way we were before we learned to spell.
And too,
connected by the faint and rooted and religious echo
of remembered flesh and blood —
the basis of ourselves together.

Come back.
I could be more,
if you could be.
I want us newly bound
by a liaison of the mind's attentiveness
to our very different selves,
and to the soul's regard for them.
I want us sitting safe and soundless
in an affair of further love.

The day is almost over,
and I need to know we have it in us,
you and I,
to be together in full honor
of our selves,
and of each other.
I need to be with you,
peaceful in our proper use,
with only that,
and all of that,
watching the last log
find a sudden flame.

PHOTO COURTESY OF PEGGY'S PERSONAL COLLECTION

TWO WIDOWS

As we sit here every Sunday evening,
and talk and drink,
and pour more vodka for you,
and pour more wine for me,
and pass the little foods on little plates,
and serious be,
inspirited by the talkative fire,
and mindful of the company of my two white cats,
who are always there,
always there...
will we,
I wonder,
we two old women with our bull-dozed lives,
ever have an answer
to the question always asked,
and never answered,
that holds us here
and doesn't let us go?

Will you and I,
I wonder,
we two women who have lost
the substance that has held our lives together,
ever find a way —
Sunday after Sunday,
Absolut after Absolut,
Chardonnay after Chardonnay —
to make our peace
with losing love?

Unexpectedly, then,
last night,
standing by the door as you were leaving,
you raised your chin,
which made you suddenly resemble
the figurehead of a sailing ship,
enduring what comes in the way of weather.
"Maybe," you said,
laughing, but serious-eyed,
"finally,
you and I will have to understand
that this is life.
And we can either take it.
Or, we can leave it,
which in a certain way
is what we're doing now."

Common sense
is as reliable
as the mixed tans and browns
of a good tweed,
loomed to give service,
and to last.
Common sense is as reliable
as the Lord's Prayer,
help of ages past.

That is what I believe
about the sanity,
and the sanctity
of common sense.
While disbelieving absolutely
that it has anything to do with the heart.

We say goodnight.
And I go back to the empty room,
and the dying fire's
apology.
My cats are there.
Cats are always there...
I pick one up,
and hold his warm and wonderful permanence
against my unemployed heart,
reviving,
for a moment,
the memory of its purpose.
It is not an ocean.
It is one of the ocean's quiet bays.
But both are the same water.

BIRTHDAY PARTY

On the sixth of March,
with red-wings trilling from the tops of trees,
four women —
long-time friends —
came to wish me happy birthday,
bringing lunch.

I had asked them,
in fact implored them,
not to bring me "things",
as gifts.
For,
in spite of what three wise men taught the world
about the sacred symbolism of the giving
of a gift,
I have always had a gut belief
that the gifts I gave
were only tokens,
were a holding back
of something primary
I was incapable of exposing.
I really knew I was not doing what came naturally,
in giving,
to my love,
at Christmas,
a little heart-shaped stone,
set in a little satin box,
and tied with silver tinsel.

And so,
on March the sixth,
there were no subterfuges to unwrap,
and oh and ah about,
no rhapsodies of gratitude
for what I did not want,

but, falsely,
said I did.
And I was spared the little sin of lying,
which takes a lot of energy.

Four long-time friends and I
sat in my sun-filled dining room
that looks beyond the pond
and finds the sea,
savoring foods they'd brought instead of tokens,
and a sparkling finale of song-borne chocolate cake,
graced with flowers from a green-house garden,
its lighted candles trembling and blowing sideways.

A red-winged blackbird sang a song
of celebration
for the newness of association.
And the sun blazed gold
in accordance with the loss of obligation.
I felt a melting innovation,
on this day of turning ninety,
and was fortified by possibilities.
Oh, to dance without grass skirts,
and make no sound of dancing!

And when I bent to blow the candles out,
I did not need to make a wish for something better.
Instead,
with one great whoosh of liberation,
I blew away the ninety years of little lies.
And then I cut the cake,
and passed it,
saying thank you.

APPOINTMENT WITH A GERONTOLOGIST

It is ten o'clock on this Friday August morning,
with reckless clouds in a wild bright sky,
and bubble-gum sails set to suck the wind,
setting forth,
setting forth...
and I am driving carefully along the harbor road,
to an appointment with a doctor
who specializes in the problems of the very old.

I am shown to an examining room,
and told to take my clothes off,
and to put on a paper gown ("gown"?)
"The Doctor will be with you shortly."
I hear her push-button, rushed, and ushering voice.

Shivering,
I put the skimpy, stiff kimono on —
white is the coldest color —
like a child's drawing of a paper doll dress.
How absurd it must look
on an old body best kept secret.

I lie down on a high, long, naugahyde-upholstered table,
and rest my arms across my coffin length.
I look up at the ceiling made of squares of styrofoam,
wishing it were the sky.
I listen to the steady sound outside
of cars going to places that are not doctor's offices,
perhaps to picnics?

The lonely door is opened
with a shocking suddenness,
and here the doctor is —
swift striding,
stethoscope hanging round his neck,
white-coated,
kind-eyed I see at once,
"What seems to be the trouble?" he asks,
taking the time to.

He smiles.
His eyes are daylight,
under the fluorescent lighting.
My breathing slows to what it's meant to be.
In seconds,
I lose one mind and find another.
Out there,
boats balloon toward open seas,
and traffic goes to picnics.
And I am in a cold, cold,
paper place.

I speak.
"You ask me, 'what seems to be the trouble?'
And I will tell you, Doctor.
There is still music in the wide, wide world.
But there is no music here."

Margaret Freydberg
P.O. Box 653
Chilmark, Ma. 02535

Mr. Richard Reston
The Vineyard Gazette
Edgartown, Ma. 02539

Dear Dick,

I'm sending you my latest poem, wondering whether you would like
it enough to consider it for the Gazette, and/or think it might
appeal to readers who are cat lovers. However, I am well aware
that it may be too long, too space-consuming. Or, that you may
not think it is appropriate, and so I am including a SASE in case
you can't use it.

However, if you do like it, and can use it comfortably,length-wise,
I wonder whether it would be within journalistic ethics, or
whether you would want to have a small line at the bottom of it,
mentioning my book, "Evening on the Pond".

In any event, my best wishes, and my great thanks for everything
you have done for me in the past.

Sincerely,

Margaret Freydberg

July, 15, 2002

A LETTER TO MY FAMILY, EXPLAINING
HOW I FEEL ABOUT MY CATS

Dearest family:

Fortunately, I can stand beside myself,
and see the gauge of my immoderate behavior
rising,
and can clearly see,
with fascination,
and without the self-reproach I ought, perhaps, to feel,
how overwrought,
how even pitiable,
my Niagara Falls of feeling for my cats
may look to you.
And I can see how you may worry
about this revelation
of starvation.

For that is what it is.
The hunger of an ancient woman's
unassuaged maternity?
Or, a hunger for the man?
Or, a longing for her kin,
who live so far away?

Yes.
All those hungers.
For all those feasts.

Yet it is something so extravagantly more,
as you will see.
And so I write to you,
with a convinced Hosannah,
with ground so solid under me,
that I am newly rooted,
newly upright.
And I proclaim to you,
I shout to you,
that I was never conscious of what I think it is to love,
until I had my two white cats.

I will explain:

One day,
as I sat looking at my cats,
I felt a new, soft, opening space
around my armor-plate of rib-cage —
like a warm wind
melting snow.
It was a feeling
of such sweet comfort,
there around my middle.
Breathing had another name.

Oh. But more than that.
For if unhappiness
feels like weights upon my chest,
and has the color of the night,
loving my cats
feels like the weights removed,
and daylight there.

And so,
with huge, benevolent laziness,
I sit and watch my cats.

I notice,
for the first time,
the way the sun shines pinkly
through their little, pointed ears.
I notice —
and with maudlin marvel —
as at the miniatureness and perfection
of a new-born baby's fingernails —
that cats have tiny eyelashes,
just like people's.

I see the beauty of their royal ermine coats,
their owl eyes,
their fluid motion —
only music,
only curves —
sparing me the jolt of human nature's sharp-edged
squares.
I watch them pounce to kill a mouse —
so soundlessly, so innocently,
so necessarily murderous.
Although I don't think murderous entirely,
I also think Pavlova and Nijinsky.

They sit and stare at me,
and wait,
and wait,
and wait,
with food-fixated eyes.
(I've come to know that look.)
Long columned legs
flow down to little paws
set so exactly,
so immaculately,
together.

Oh little lovely cats,
pouncing to devour so ravenously
the food that I've put down for you.
I wish you did not need to be dependent,
you of such heroic independence.
How do you keep your excellence,
your equanimity,
when all you do
is wait,
and wait,
and wait,
for what you need?
How do you settle for subordination,
with such grandeur?

It comes to me,
that what has made my looking,
loving,
is not the limbic lilt of seeing beauty,
though that is there.
It is the recognition of the character of a cat,
which is so anciently,
so perseveringly,
so unchangingly,
substantial —
Darwin's fittest.
In two white cats

I see the grace
of being what one knows one is,
and having it suffice eternally.

And I,
to be so old,
to be so new —
a luxurious lack of interest in the overlay of
me
on what it is I'm looking at,
lies now on me like loosened harnessing.
If breathing has another word,
then so does seeing.
I am focused on the knowing of a cat.

And so I end this letter to my family:

Come stay with me,
and be my loves.
Then I can love my cat
with temperance;
and all of you,
the way that watching two white cats
has taught me to.

ATTITUDES

Why do I go on and on
about the heart grief of old widows?
Why must I kneel with all the other black-shawled ancients
who beat their heads against that wailing wall,
and wallow in its communal dark drowning?

Why do I describe so piteously to you,
the pop-corn solitude of an old woman's aloneness
in a movie on a Sunday afternoon?
And the disappointment of lilacs?
And that dawn,
and spring,
are harder to believe in?

What is left,
I mourn,
besides my blood that flows,
imperfectly,
through faithful arteries?
Sift through the wreckage of myself
that cannot be rebuilt,
rake through the bones and dust
of empty rooms,
to see if there is something still alive in there,
that once belonged to me.

. . . . .

One morning,
I awake
to the novelty of a mind
washed pale and clear as early dawn.
And with the thought
that I have done with my complaining,
which allows no attitude but its own.
I sense a sudden spartan splendor
in a knowing
that is not a feeling.

Where is the music of my wailing —
my only steady company?
I cannot hear it
for the sound that thinking makes.

And so,
with sensibilities de-emphasized,
I turn to sense.
I turn to lonely, lonely,
bleak, but vitalizing
common sense.
It is like cold fresh air.

It's true,
of course,
that I am permanently altered,
and that sorrowing grows deeper,
more internal.
There is no way I do not know that this is so.

Yet I can see,
that there can be,
a safe sublimity
in feeling,
for the first time in a long time,
reasonable;
that there can be
eternity,
in simply saying,
"That's the way it is,"
voicing the peace and order
of the facts.

SURVIVAL OF THE FITTEST

I like to think it matters to the lilac
that my face is thrust into its gloss of heaven,
and that,
shone upon,
I am persuaded once again,
that bliss is not imaginary;
and that this lilac bliss I breathe
does, actually, exist;
created by evolution for this purpose.

A lavender cloud beside old doorstep in country fields
the houses gone.
The lilacs stay,
recurrent as the air of spring,
giving its message to my breathing.

I like to think it matters to the lilac
that its evolutionary purpose
is to tease me,
seize me,
for a moment's recognition
that what its nascent sweetness is,
exists.
Its sky-high, tantalizing
inconceivability,
exists,
reminding me
how unprepared I am
to die unpolished by what it is the lilac promises.

NECESSARY CONJUNCTION

I have turned to look at him.
We are sitting together,
having breakfast,
in the code of congruence
known only to a man and woman married many years.

And all at once,
I see his hand.
A loose fist of fingers,
lying very still,
by itself.
Inert beside his empty coffee cup.

At this same instant,
I see that this is what my loving him
boils down to:
not great things clamoring for remembrance —
the moments of infinity we brought to loving;
or the calm, substantial truth of
bodies lying side by side in sleep.
And not the everything of two lives
being one, for half a life-time.
Just his hand.

I have always known,
and told him,
that I love his hands —
the marvel of their maleness,
the essence,
and the testament,
of all the manlihood that fleshed my life —
strong and beautiful blunt fingers,
that gripped the tiller of his schooner in a gale;
that grabbed my elbow when I slipped on ice;
that stroked his cat along its back as gently
as the faintest breeze.

Male and female.
Necessary conjunction.
How new was maleness when it came to me.
It was another kind of blood that filled my arteries —
his ready blood,
my readiness to be transfused by it —
bringing equilibrium.
How wonderfully,
how unexpectedly,
it filled my being.
Changed it.
Created me as woman.

. . . . .

I am old, and I am cold. And he is gone.
I am covered in a great outdoors frigidity,
and hard as ice.
Unfleshed.

I have a glitter of a life,
genuine in endeavor to survive alone,
scrupulous in undertaking,
"successful" in the eyes of all who marvel
at nonagenarian accomplishment.
Unyielding as I never was before he died.

But what is left of softness
beneath the armor of my altered self,
encasing me,
replacing me?
I never do the things I used to love to do
so carelessly and so contentedly —
take walks and pick the first arbutus,
play music all day long,
dress up for dinner with a string of pearls.

Where is what was soft?
Where is the unplanned walk
to find a lady-slipper in the woods,
in spring?

The title "Necessary Conjunction" is from T.S. Eliot's Four Quartets, "East Coker."

BLIZZARD

It takes courage to see beauty
in a world spread deep and silent
with interminable whiteness;
and to keep on being awed
by such uncommon splendor
while trying to suppress
a fundamental fear
of being buried by it.

But know it as it is:
Beauty is everlasting.
And winter's burial is not.
Underneath cold winter bone,
the flesh of summer sleeps.

BE STILL, MY SOUL

The rooms overlooking the pond
have enlarged with an ethereal light.
The sky fills them.

It is time to light a fire,
to pour a glass of wine.
To sit,
and wait,
for all those satisfactions
that always fail to satisfy.

Instead,
restless, I start to wander
through the strange vast glowing of the rooms.
I tell myself
I want to see the hymn of setting sun
along the old stone wall built centuries ago
to keep a farmer's sheep from wandering far afield.

By a window in the bedroom,
on an antique carved Italian chair,
I find my cat,
sitting with unfathomable stillness,
looking out.

At what?
I see no creature moving.
But,
how can I see
what cats see?
How can I perceive a variation of existence
known only to a cat,
who watches the light on an old stone wall,
or the ghosts of sheep?

For my soul's sake,
I bend,
and,
carefully,
I place the palms of both my hands
along his sides,
finding a being without boundaries.

Sudden,
complete and sweet as truth,
his stillness
strikes me into stillness.

The title is from a song by Katharina Von Schlegel, born 1697.

PHOTO COURTESY OF YANN MEERSSEMAN / VINEYARD COLORS

WAIT A MINUTE

I open my eyes in the morning.
For a minute
I am neither here nor there.
Then in the next minute
I am here but starting
to be there.

The day has begun.

I will get up
and start to seek,
and continue starting,
so that every minute of this day
will begin with an anticipation
of the promise of the next one.
All day long and into the evening,
every minute of my waking hours,
I will not be here
because I am seeking
to be there.

I tell myself —
a pill will do it,
a walk in the fine fresh air will do it,
a Villa-Lobos prelude will do it,
a message on my telephone answering machine will do it,
a good library book will do it,
a glass of white wine at five o'clock will do it,
a good dinner will do it.

I close my eyes in the evening,
and I say to myself,
with relief at the day's ending:
a good night's sleep will do it.

Every day is the same.
I never stop to ask:
"Do what?"
I never think to look for
what it is
that lies between the
beginning of the minute
and the end of it.

THE DANCE

Here I stand,
in a long, loose dress that covers imperfections,
looking through the glass wall of the room,
to the dazzling and complete perfection of the sea,
considering the contradiction of what lasts,
and what does not,
and asking the sea if there is any better way to think,
or any better way to feel,
about what ends?

All the objects in this room behind me,
once a part of the dance of him and me,
now seem as motionless
as their reflection in the wall of glass.
What does the melodious grand piano have to do
with the old woman, as finished as the keyboard never tuned,
who does not play it for him any more,
who flings a helpless but still questioning hand
toward the sea that never ages,
wanting to know about what endures,
and how to live with what does not?

Remember the wallflower,
the only girl in the row of chairs around the dance floor,
sitting with her hoping heart
beneath the cold stiff taffeta's rustling invitation,
waiting for a boy to come along,
and bow,
and take her hand,
and lead her to the center,
where the dance is.

All the time,
these days,
standing by the closed piano,
and the pale polaroid stillness of a flowering hibiscus
reflected in the wall of glass,
I ask the sea to tell me
whether there is any way to live
with the broken-function years
of being very old?

Can I find peace,
find being,
in the peripheral existence of an old woman?
Must I surrender to the contradiction
of an imperishable sea and my impermanence,
and the fate of being very old,
and solitary,
and so, unharboured?

Looking to the sea that does not answer,
I find the answer,
coming from the oracle within — the only place that knows;
for what the sea tells me, is what I have already told the sea.
And so,
to it I give this answer I have found,
because I want the everlasting sea to know
what I, with sudden clearness,
know is everlasting, too:

An old woman,
in a long, loose dress that covers imperfections,
is sitting in a row of empty chairs reserved for wallflowers,
hoping, though she fears it may not happen,
that an old man,
someone she has never known,
will come along,
and stop before her chair,
and bow,
and take her hand in both of his,
asking for the last dance.

TRANSFORMATION

The eyes of a very wise old woman,
whose face was once her fortune,
tell you that she knows
her flesh can only be considered
as something loose that hangs on bones,
and in the service,
now,
of nothing but the truth
of being old.

Her eyes disclose,
with gallantry in control,
that she is still attempting
to forget about her face —
the only way to deal with what she sees
as an absurdity,
and which she chooses not to have smoothed flat
by knives and stitches.

In her eyes
there is a deadly patience
with the ruination of what was,
and must,
for balance,
be condoned.
Bleak, serviceable,
wearily amused and even interested,
her eyes inform you of how strange it is,
how, even, liberating,
to have lived through transformation;

to have understood,
and so,
to have withstood,
to some extent,
the helplessness of being ancient,
and without a face
as she has known a face.
And if this very wise old woman
seems beautiful,
(as some say aging faces often are),
it may be so,
for she is still a striking sight,
with hair as white as swans on water,
and with grey eyes, steely brave,
daring you to see
old flesh in all its shame,
and willing you to know
it must be borne.

But do not tell her
that her face is beautiful.
For she will answer,
with her eyes,
that she knows what she is,
at last,
and it is not her face
has made her so.
She does not want to hear the sound of praise,
again,
and be twice fooled.

Compulsively,
I strive to find a method
for a confrontation with what must be done
to save my children from the task of doing it when I die.
Make lists.
Make lists.
I sharpen pencils with an out-damn-spot intensity.
In shaded rooms,
on yellow pads,
I hide myself from sun
to settle my affairs:
"The Steuben heart of glass, though chipped,
will go to Bet, who never scolds imperfect hearts."
"The primitive I painted years ago,
while sitting in a field behind the house,
will go to Jocelyn, who understands it was
the first day of my life I saw what I was looking at."
Clean out the attic,
go through the endless drawers of files,
spend what little time is left to me
in scuttling all the props
on table tops,
and all the evidence of the "getting and the spending
that laid waste my powers..."

But?
Must I throw the stack of twenty journal-notebooks
in the trash,
with no mind for the dignity
of the burial of my secrets?

      All at once,
      answering myself,
      I sit tiredly in the emptied room,
      cold in the evening light.
      I have forgotten to light a fire.
      There is no color of a flame.
      I am in a large white death.

Go back.
Live with my mistakes.
Leave my clutter.
After I am gone,
when those of you who loved me
walk in this room,
you will find,
to your surprise
that I'm still here.

RESTORATION

On impulse,
I began to read,
again,
a novel I had written,
long ago.

Once having started it,
I could not stop.
The turning of each page brought awe,
for I saw there
full bloom of me who once observed each blade of grass,
each mountain,
and was compelled to bring this into words
to try to match such beauty;
who saw and understood
each lifted eyebrow,
each heart confused, rejoicing, stricken.
All this I saw,
in shock,
and wonder,
and then,
in sudden slaughtering disbelief.

How could I have seen this,
thought this,
felt this?
How could I have written such a book?
And what remained
of me who made this book so many years ago?
And was there anything in 99's infirmity,
that justified ongoingness,
now that creativity had ended?

. . . . .

I stayed in this condition
of being blown to bits
for days
for weeks.
No pill,
no Hospice-like encouragement from
counselor, or family, or friends,
restored to me
the loss of what I once had been.
The life I'd once observed so plentifully,
the nutriment of being that observer,
of being the partaker of the whole of the fruit,
was gone.
And thus,
abandoned by identity,
I was ended.

So what was there to live on,
between now,
and finally,
then?

. . . . .

But live I must.
Of course.
And finally
pushed towards restoration
by the growing will to be restored,
and by a feeling in the center of my forehead,
contained within a clear-edged mass
of something dense but without form,
like smoke,
awaiting transformation
into what was there to know —
finally,
I picked up yellow pad and yellow pencil.
And I began to write:
      A Poem.
      Born to clarify.
      The first of those to come.

      And here it is.

Interview at 95

"Peggy Freydberg, Who Dwells in the Present"
By C.K. Wolfson
Printed in the Vineyard Gazette – Sept. 19, 2003

The afternoon will be sipped, not gulped; tea served in china cups and saucers; considered words; a hovering calm. Everything will happen in its own unrushed moment, and the ordinary will take on the air of occasion.

Poet and author Margaret (Peggy) Howe Freydberg, wearing a full skirt, cardigan sweater over her blouse and city shoes, sits erect and rather formally on one of the two long couches on either side of the fireplace. Behind her the sky is seeping into Stonewall Pond. Her Chilmark living room is an interior landscape in shades of beige; nothing random, sea shells, heart-shaped rocks, original art, family photographs, all assembled with a poet's discrimination. Even the blossoms of the large flowering tree in the floor pot seem deliberately arranged for aesthetic effect.

Mrs. Freydberg, sounding and looking 20 years younger than her 95 years, is reflecting on age: "I think it's two things. It's deterioration and disorientation, and multiple losses: physical, emotional, mental."

Speaking thoughtfully and fluently, she first measures her words, then lets her voice run the scale. "It's very, very hard, and nobody needs to be told that. But – and I think this is very universal – there's an increase in the use of the heart and a beauty and comfort and eternalness in nature, and those get intensified."

Mrs. Freydberg, as warm and welcoming as she is genteel, has published five novels, a memoir (Growing Up in Old Age, Parnassus Imprint, 1998), and a self-published book of poetry (Evening On The Pond, Brook House, 2001). And between introductions and small talk, she casually serves up succinct bits of life wisdom, like conversational hors d'ouevres.

"The only right is the right you are confident about inwardly," she says sounding almost offhanded. "I've lived so long with doing the 'right' things."

There's a hint of a sigh when she says she wishes she had learned earlier to express herself verbally with spontaneous clarity. "Being a writer I can express what I really mean, but I don't have the quick mind to put it together fast enough to say the right thing." She smiles a dowager's smile, and pauses to murmur affectionately to one of the two cats prowling nearby.

Tea is served with bits of personal Then and Now: her first husband, the late publisher Samuel Sloan, brought her into contact with such literary figures as Wallace Stegner and John O'Hara; she enjoys a close relationship with her two children, seven grandchildren and four great-grandchildren; she writes in longhand; and, after asserting that she's "not wacky," adds, "Cats have become one of the most important things in my life."

In the course of her life she has endured what she refers to as a lot of tragedy, but admits, "I think I have some miraculous capacity to bury it." When she finds herself approaching the boundary of a topic she doesn't want to pursue, she abruptly interrupts herself: "Never mind, let's not talk about that," or, "That's a whole story in itself," and changes the subject.

Topics drift from particulars to generalities, life lessons and philosophy, then close in on writing. And threaded through each are the glancing references to her husband of 40 years, publisher (co-founder of Basic Books) and social psychologist Nicholas Freydberg, who died nine years ago on July 14.

"And I thought, 'Revolution,'" she says. "And

it was such a revolution to be alone at 80. Nobody's prepared for that."

She admits, "I wrote Growing Up in Old Age because I was so afraid of dying. And I knew that I was controlled by fear. It is very constricting and destructive to always be living beyond the moment; to be preparing. I found the answer was to live in the present and not keep thinking about the future. It's just so hard. You can't tell yourself to feel one way. It's very much of a Buddhist thing – not permitting extraneous thought, fears and prejudices and the minutia that has nothing to do with the present. If you're [not thinking about] yourself, you're in the present." She smiles. "Watching a cat is staying in the moment."

My energies go into writing. Writing is an absolute need: the need to express myself and to express the experience. Nick never understood why I needed to be published. He thought that writing itself ought to be enough. Well, if I never thought I was going to be published, I'm sure I would write anyway. But I don't think that the work that you've done is ever complete until it's been received. If you have something that you feel is of value, and

IT IS VERY CONSTRICTING AND DESTRUCTIVE TO ALWAYS BE LIVING BEYOND THE MOMENT; TO BE PREPARING. I FOUND THE ANSWER WAS TO LIVE IN THE PRESENT AND NOT KEEP THINKING ABOUT THE FUTURE.

you can really respect it and know it's trying to be art… I think Nick was wrong. Look at what art has done for the world."

Turning from prose to poetry was less a decision than Mrs. Freydberg's need to express herself, "and it turned out that poetry was the way to do it, because it's just wonderful in terms of finding out what you don't know. It's so distilled. I don't think I can explain it.

I write to find out what I don't know. You know what I mean. Anybody can do it. The glory and the challenge of poetry is finding exactly what you want to say."

"When you think of what the brain is capable of, and what you feel you might be capable of, you just don't want it to end." Mrs. Freydberg laughs lightly. "It's the great human potential."

Growing Up in Old Age

Excerpts from the Memoir

"In the core of everything is the truth of it"

ON GROWING OLD

I know that growing old is like finding yourself, surprisingly and disturbingly, in a country that is foreign to you…

Suddenly you realize that you are here, in a strange place, and that here you will, without any way of going back, be staying.

As you stand alone on this barren plain, your single shadow lying long and black across its late afternoon light, you realize that this new country is bleak and it is lonely, and is without reference to anything you have ever known.

Nothing much terrible has happened to you yet, just little things. But terrible things are happening all the time to others and may happen to you too.

You are at last, admittedly, full of fear.

I tell myself that I must see something in the mirror besides my wrinkled veneer if I am to have any calm; that I will have to make my peace with the loss of smooth skin, and find satisfaction in the gaining of something to take its place. Something, yes, that should always have been in me. Or something that has always been in me but has never seen the light of day.

And so I stand in this open countryside where there are no familiar landmarks, and it comes to me suddenly that, yes, this is the country of old age.

I am old. What's more, I accept the reality, humbling though the thought is, that people will look at me and see that I am old.

It has gone, that mindless safety, so blissful while it lasted, of believing that it couldn't happen to me. It has gone.

ON HAPPINESS

My own happiness – I can even call it joy – is the passion of looking at and reacting to and assimilating the life of this earth. It derives from such commonplace things as breathing sea air, setting one foot in front of the other, feeling well, hearing birds sounding, getting into a car and starting it up to go somewhere, thinking back on the events of the day before and knowing that even though they were unremarkable I would love to live them over again. In Cronig's Market yesterday, everything about it, everything my eyes saw and my hands did, felt memorable and desirable and worth doing over again.

ON WORRY

I am learning something very important as I go along. It is that even if there is a likelihood of the worst coming to pass, I still cannot be certain that it will. Many, many times in my life there have been serious crises, but none of them ever had any resemblance to my preview of them.

…by trying to live through the worst possible imagined situations that can occur, if perchance they do occur, I have managed to make myself live through them twice – once in imagination, once in actuality. Oh how I waste my time!

Am I to spend the remainder of my life in the wasteful grip of the fear of the loss of it? The answer I give myself is no – a very decided no. Because worry… is now absolutely unacceptable to me, and I am sick of it.

ON WHAT CAN BE LOST

My looks
Material conditions
People
Minor talents and accomplishments
Ability to write

ON WHAT CAN REMAIN

My life force
My integrity
My heart
My love of nature
My values
My inmost being

It is clear that those conditions, talents, social satisfactions – do not appear to be substantial bases for the pursuit of happiness in old age, since they are more than likely to go.

But those qualities that could survive and are not predictably subject to change, could be it seems to me, reliable bases for essential living. Indispensable to the pursuit of happiness and to happiness itself, those are the qualities, I believe, from which courage could come.

ON WRITING

Writing is my chief, conscious way of finding out what I didn't know I knew, of bringing together observations, information and experience stored up in me and processed in there and often delivered eventually as discovery.

Writing, for me, has always been a search, a sense of ongoingness, a sense of not standing still. I recommend it to anyone who can hold a pencil or use a typewriter or speak into a tape recorder.

ON WONDER

One day I had a momentary, sharp sense of how remarkable it would be to have a way of viewing crows and snow-covered fields without such needy, such self-located eyes. Wouldn't it be a new and unusually interesting experience, I thought with excitement, to look at a world that is not filtered by me, that loses me in the looking?

I looked at the sea. And in looking at it, all at once I saw the fact of it, the life within it, and the rock I was sitting on, a part of it, I saw warm living shore, cold living sea, and for the moment, detached from my own involvement in earth and sea, I had an illumination of the oneness and the counterpoint of life. And in seeing this I had such a strong sense of life – not a feeling about it but an attentive comprehending of it – that I was taken out of myself in a calm, sensible way. Life is, I thought, with a sober thrill. It is not as I see it, but as it is.

ON FEAR

I am determined not to let the fear of growing old deprive me of the happiness that has always come naturally to me.

Fear is not new to me, not something that has suddenly appeared in my old age. I have always been "anxiety prone." …And so now, inevitably I suppose, in this new and foreign country of old age, fear has become an active and pervasive emotion that often disturbs my days and witches my nights.

I hate it because it is so unassailable. I hate it because it is so unreasonable. I hate it most of all because I know that what I am feeling is not specifically a fear of illness, or aging or of death or of any other disasters… but the fear of fear.

And so at the end of this book that has been a search to find the meaning of the fear of old age and a solution to the lessening of it, I ask myself, "where is fear now?"

And I answer, "Fear is where I let it be."

ON SELF ESTEEM

And all the time, at bottom what I really craved was to be recognized not primarily for my appearance but profoundly and longingly, even pathetically, for something in me that knew better – my mind, my true spirit, my integrity – that part of me that had had such a hard time seeing the light of day.

I know my values and that I have an innocent passion for decency, a rage to be decent, to want others to be decent, to want the world to be decent. So I know myself to be, innately, a decent person.

ON MARTHA'S VINEYARD

The material conditions of my life are this beautiful Island; the sea; the fields around the house; the pond below it; the brook running beside it; the comfortable, agreeable house itself; its furnishings; its music; its books; its kitchen; its food; its sun-filled rooms. And seventy-five miles away, the fine old city of Boston.

PHOTO COURTESY OF PEGGY'S PERSONAL COLLECTION

An Unofficial Biography

Margaret Howe Freydberg was born March 6, 1908 in Rochester, New York. She was the middle of three children. Both her siblings suffered from degenerative eye disease. Her sister was born blind and her brother eventually lost his sight in his twenties. As a result, she grew up in a house "drenched in a sense of melancholy." Strict Protestant values and an oppressive religious environment defined her childhood. She describes her early years as filled with guilt and fear. "Thinking about what I had that my sister didn't was the refrain that I grew up with," she remembers. (See "The Final Change," page 31.) "Fear pervaded my life but it never touched my spirit, which was sparkling," she confides.

Peggy's first marriage was to Sam Sloan, a literary man whose gifts as an editor and publisher helped him establish the publishing company Duell, Sloan and Pearce in 1939. His charm and abilities attracted some of the top talent of the day including MFK Fisher, John O'Hara, Archibald MacLeish, Erskine Caldwell, Wallace Stegner, e.e. cummings, Howard Fast, Benjamin Spock, and Conrad Aiken. The Sloans lived in Paris for two years building Sam's roster of French authors and on return to New York, enjoyed a stimulating literary social life.

Judging from condolence letters written to Peggy after Sam's untimely death (complications from hip surgery) in 1945, it was apparent that his authors cared deeply for him as a friend, a gifted and tenacious editor, and an inventive publisher. Peggy often described him as "elegant."

Two children came from this first marriage – a son named Sam and a daughter named Laidily. Between them they gave Peggy eight wonderful grandchildren.

PEGGY AND SAM
PHOTO COURTESY OF PEGGY'S PERSONAL COLLECTION

PEGGY AND NICK
PHOTO COURTESY OF PEGGY'S PERSONAL COLLECTION

Peggy remarried several years later to Nicholas Freydberg, also a member of the literati and co-founder of Basic Books, specializing in psychology, sociology, economics, philosophy, and politics. A graduate of the University of Pennsylvania, Nicholas went back to school in his mid-fifties and received a Ph.D. in social psychology from New York University.

In addition to his publishing accomplishments Nick was an avid environmentalist, sailor, and intellect. In 1982 he co-authored the comprehensive The Food Additive Book, which was published by Bantam and served as a prescient warning on the dangerous chemicals found in our food.

Peggy details her long love affair with Nick in all of her writings (see "Call Me but Love and I'll Be New Baptized," page 36) and characterizes their relationship as "inseparable" for 47 years. Her writings extol her love for him but she also laments his "quiet nature," her "all-encompassing" commitment to being his wife, and the difficulties of finding her own true self within the marriage. His many friends described him as "a grand gentleman and a gifted human being."

Their love of Martha's Vineyard brought them year round to the Island in 1969 where they retired to a classic beach house nestled on the edge of Stonewall Pond. Nick worked on local conservation issues and Peggy wrote several novels in a writing tent Nick set up for her on their lawn. Here she penned the groundbreaking memoir, Growing Up in Old Age, which courageously confronted her fear of dying, asking the question, "Am I to spend the rest of my life in the fear of losing it?"

Peggy tackled the universal themes of aging head on and came up with some important conclusions. "I tell myself that I must see something in the mirror besides my wrinkled veneer if I am to have any calm; that I will have to make my peace with the loss of smooth skin, and find satisfaction in the gaining of something to take its place."

It was while writing this memoir that her beloved Nick passed away at 87.

Peggy, desperate to continue expressing herself and no longer able to write long form, began to write the poems in this collection. She was just entering her 90th year.

She described the day it occurred to her to write poetry as, "A force that had lodged in my head and demanded to come out." (See "Restoration," page 92.)

Peggy continues to reside with a treasured cat (see "A letter to My Family, Explaining How I Feel About My Cats," page 67) in her home on Stonewall Pond. A small glass of white wine is ritually enjoyed at five p.m. in front of her fire and friends and family visit regularly.

The wheels driving her to understand herself and confront her fears continue to spin. It's an essential key to her longevity… that and dark chocolate, she suggests. She is still searching for answers to life's simple and complex questions.

Peggy is currently 107 years old.

PEGGY, NICK AND THEIR EXTENDED FAMILY
PHOTO COURTESY OF PEGGY'S PERSONAL COLLECTION

PEGGY WITH HER GREAT-GRANDDAUGHTER ZIVAH SOLOMON
PHOTO COURTESY OF EMILY SLOAN

Afterword

My love for my grandmother began very early. If I had to pinpoint it I would say it started around age 10 when I was just beginning to be aware that I was an independent and free-flowing being, despite the fact that the grownups surrounding me seemed to think otherwise. I was used to adults looking through me, asking me questions as their eyes shifted onto another object and their thoughts drifted onto something else before they were even done with, "How is school, dear?" Not Gran. It was so shocking to me initially that I almost felt like I should turn my head to see who was standing behind me. She was really seeing me and I remember feeling startled, honored, and excited. My grandparents' house became my favorite retreat; my safe place.

As I grew older and my grandfather got sick and eventually passed away, I felt such tremendous loss. I was terrified my grandmother might quickly follow and disappear from my life too. When I would visit, I would stare at her as if I could etch her image into my brain just in case I never saw her again. I think this practice started when she was in her early-80s and continued into her 90s. It was probably somewhere in her mid-90s that I stopped doing it. I realized she was forever etched in my brain. Ironically, she wasn't showing any

signs of dying soon. In fact she seemed to be getting younger and more creative and more vibrant the older she got.

My Gran had her share of challenges growing up. She was raised in a strict religious household, with an authoritarian father and a distant mother who was consumed with her role as a caregiver for her blind sister. My grandmother once told me that she felt like she simply didn't exist in her mother's eyes. The responsibility of being the "healthy" daughter amidst the tragedy of two visually impaired siblings weighed heavily on her.

Gran was (and still is) uncommonly beautiful, but as much as her beauty opened doors, it also felt oppressive to her in conjunction with the societal demands of women in the early 1900's. She felt pressure to be perfect inside and out, cause no trouble, make no waves, be admired, and be seen but not heard.

She was sent to "finishing school" where "Dobb's girls" were taught to be modest and "to live useful, orderly lives, based on truthfulness, integrity, and responsibility." She struggled all her life with the assumption (hers and others) that there was no mind inside her worth sharing, no voice worth using.

But she broke free of that at a time when other women seemed content to remain powerless. She poured her struggles into five novels where she questioned issues of self and identity, gender, and society.

My grandmother has always been incredibly graceful, elegantly dressed, and conscious of her clothing, her jewelry, her environment.

She's the kind of charming that is magical, almost like royalty, and at the same time, a few times, we did hear her swear like a sailor. Mostly it was with family as an expression of pure outrage against some indignity or injustice, but once, she wielded her shillelagh and told a police officer who stopped her for speeding, "I hate you!" He was reportedly "dumbstruck" and didn't give her a ticket. Generally, she is the epitome of grace and kindness.

Gran's writing has always been about the search. Decades ago she quietly explored Taoism, spirituality, and living in the moment way before it became the chic buzzwords of our culture. She read Jon Kabat-Zinn, and Alan Watts and practiced what she learned.

It must be genetic. I, too, search and question and wonder and noodle to death things that might better be left untouched. It's one thing to seek answers in the first half of your life, but to be continuing to expand and explore at 107 is remarkable.

One of her poems entitled "Blizzard" sits on my wall for that one line – "underneath cold winter bone, the flesh of summer sleeps." To me that has always meant that we can march on with our external body, our skeleton, our exterior lives, doing one thing, maybe doing what we have to, but we should never forget that underneath it all, opportunity can be awakened at any time. It's always there for all of us, at any age.

When I think about what she's accomplished writing novels in her 50s, 60s, and 70s, a deep and soul searching memoir in her 80s, turning to poetry in her 90s and continuing to write more poetry into her 100s – you realize that the opportunities are out there if you break free. She is the epitome of the phrase *anything is possible*.

People often ask me to describe my Gran, and I usually say: My grandmother... my grandmother is the kind of person who will walk outside and bend and sniff the lilacs and call me up and exclaim, "Oh Tamara, have you smelled the lilacs? They're so heavenly!"

Above all I think one of the shining qualities about my grandmother is her kindness. As a child you could pluck a clover flower in the grass, mangle it in your sweaty palms and hand it to her with a stone and she would look you in the eyes and tell you that this was the most incredible gift that she has ever received. And you would believe it because you knew that in that moment in time she believed it too.

Surprisingly, Gran has always harbored doubts about how much she has been loved by her husband and those around her. I remember clearly sitting in the library with my grandfather in one of those quiet moments we used to have where we discussed books, my schooling, my life – and my grandmother padding down the hall, long skirt swishing, passing by the open door of the library – my grandfather, in his quiet, intense manner, with his legs crossed, his long elegant fingers folded on his knees, said to me, (uncharacteristically, because he was a very cerebral man) – "she doesn't know how much I love her."

She really didn't know and I want to remind her – with these words that she was loved very, very deeply by her husband and is loved very, very deeply by her family.

I would like to convey my heartfelt gratitude to Nancy Aronie and Laurie David for recognizing my grandmother as the gem that she is, daring to envision this project, and so quickly acting on their vision to produce this beautiful book and send it flying out into the world. Without their commitment, my beloved grandmother would have remained a secret to a small circle of admirers. This book is a testament to her brilliance and an inspiration to women everywhere.

Tamara Sloan

PEGGY WITH TAMARA AND FAMILY
PHOTO COURTESY OF JULIE JAFFEE

"Gran means more to me than words can express. She inspires, supports, acknowledges and provides unconditional love to her great-grandchildren, Zivah and Hunter, and me. Gran is poetry."

Emily Sloan

OTHER PUBLISHED WORKS
by Margaret Howe Freydberg

The Bride
Harper, 1952

The Lovely April
Scribner, 1955

Winter Concert
Backcountry Publishing, 1985

Katherine's House
Countryman Press, 1986

The Consequences of Loving Syra
Countryman Press, 1990

Growing Up in Old Age
Parnassus Imprints, 1998

The following poems have been published in the Vineyard Gazette:
"The Allen Farm" *March 17, 2000*
"Chorus of Cells" *February 16, 2001*
"Of Two Minds" *May 18, 2001*
"The Swimming Lesson" *September 14, 2001*
"Holding Macalistair" *March 8, 2002*
"Come Stay with Me and My Two White Cats" *August 16, 2002*
"Blizzard" *March 7, 2003*
"Getting There" *October 10, 2003*
"Resurrection" *February 6, 2004*
"But Where is What I Started For, so Long Ago, and Why is it Yet Unfound?" *November 19, 2004*
"Appointment with a Gerontologist" *May 13, 2005*
"Survival of the Fittest" *May 23, 2008*
"Mornings at Seven" *August 8, 2008*
"Message to a Widow" *December 19, 2008*
"Preparing Oneself for Dying" *September 4, 2009*
"Making Sure" *March 5, 2010*

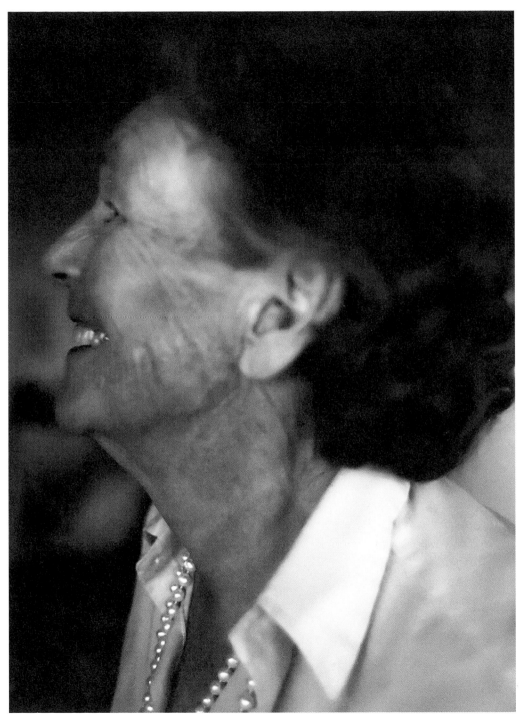

PHOTO COURTESY OF PEGGY'S PERSONAL COLLECTION

FOR MARGARET HOWE FREYDBERG, WRITER ON THE OCCASION OF HER 100TH BIRTHDAY

Tell all the truth but tell it slant . . .
The truth must dazzle gradually
Or every man be blind.
Emily Dickinson

There's no metaphor for a life in writing, evening
on the pond, where the pasture dips to the dunes,
the tide drawing Katherine under, pulling a line
to let the wind catch canvas on Daughter of Dove,
or turning a word over and over on the shore to find
the smooth side and the light, the heart in the sunset.

She writes, if it were not for the light, would I see
layers. No tenure, just the deep wish to know what
endures, to get it right, what strikes her into stillness,
what makes life right, beyond all her dreamings,
wonderful. Every day there are places you have to go,
the bed you have to make, each morning stung by joy.

She drives to the library, mails a letter, feeds her cats —
the words continue, she continues, the swimmers weightless
in the water, pushing through ferocious riches, endless jewels
rolling off their shoulders, plunging into bursts of brilliance,
a basilica filled with women returning from a masquerade
in blue and green gowns, silver earrings created from light

on water, tiny filings from stars. It's opulence as they dip
their arms in long strokes, as stone and sea glass rattle
and recede. She begins again — looking through to water,
rough and raging grays, frozen sea smoke, novels and poems
continue, the walk to the unknown, the push to understand
tigers and strawberries, what lies between the beginning

of the minute and the end of it — seven moonstones
and smaller yellow diamonds, music in the wide,
wide world, amber flicker from the light of the fire,
and the importance of all things unsaid, passing
little foods on little plates, finding love —
a red-winged blackbird sings a song of celebration.

John Maloney

BIRTHDAY CELEBRATION AT THE CHILMARK LIBRARY
PHOTO COURTESY OF THE VINEYARD GAZETTE AND MARK LOVEWELL

Acknowledgements

To say this book was a labor of love would be a serious understatement. Nancy and I fell madly in love with Peggy and her poems and this book was quickly born out of that passion and admiration. It wasn't long before we realized we weren't alone in that sentiment. Everyone we approached to contribute to this book did so happily and with deep respect for Peggy.

On that list are the photographers who have so generously contributed their pictures. Our thanks go out to Vineyard Gazette photographer Mark Lovewell, Vineyard Colors, Lynn Christoffers, Julie Jaffee, and Peggy's granddaughter, Emily Sloan. Vineyarder Eli Dagostino (whose gorgeous photograph adorns the cover) took his shots during his Thanksgiving break and Vineyard Colors founder Yann Meersseman, in addition to going through his archival footage of Stonewall Pond, went back to the site at the crack of dawn several times, waiting for the perfect sunrise.

Thank you to Peggy's family who opened their scrapbooks and shared their memories. Special thanks to Peggy's granddaughter Tamara Sloan for her contributions and for so lovingly guiding us through Peggy's life. Thank you to Peggy's son Sam Sloan for sharing his stories and for the memorable cocktail celebration in front of Peggy's treasured fireplace on a cold, Vineyard day. A glass of champagne never tasted better.

Thank you to my associate Dawn Woollen who has handled all the logistics involved with this project with her usual grace, competency, and professionalism. And many thanks to Jessica Roddy who initially invited me to attend the poetry reading at Nancy's studio and has helped with this project. Thank you Amy Lennard Goehner for her keen eye and love of grammar.

Many thanks to ICLA and the great job they did printing this book. Thank you David Humphrey for immediately understanding what we were trying to accomplish and for bringing in his top designer, April Lizardo. April took this manuscript and turned it into the beautiful book you are now holding. (In record time!) Thank you sweet James Hill for putting us in such good hands.

Thank you is also due the venerable Vineyard Gazette for recognizing Peggy's talents long ago and printing many of her poems for Island readers. Thank you Hilary Wall for the archival help! Also, our deep appreciation goes to another Vineyard institution, the Chilmark Library, with special thanks to Kristen Maloney and Ebba Hierta for supporting

Peggy's insatiable literary appetite all these years. Our local library also gets kudos for organizing the wonderful 100th birthday bash for Peggy. It was for this celebration that poet John Maloney wrote his ode to her in his inimitable style, cleverly weaving many of Peggy's actual words from her body of work into his verse. Thank you John for allowing us to reprint it here.

There are many people who have loved and cared for Peggy and who made it possible for her to focus on her writing and the parts of her life that bring her pleasure. Oceans of thanks from her family to all of them, with a special shout-out to Linda Alley, Lauri Bradway, Chris Cull, Debbie Giuffre, John Maloney, Donald and Pat Malonson, Wendy Marzbanian, Pat Phelan, Maribeth Priore, Richard Santos, Denise Walsh, Emily Weatherall, Karen Wilson and Charles (Chip) Young.

Peggy has also been blessed with great friends and even better neighbors and she would like to thank three very close to her heart: Betsy Cornwall and Julie and Miles Jaffee.

Encouragement for this book came from a few very special friends, Pulitzer Prize-winning author Geraldine Brooks, two-term Poet Laureate Billy Collins, and author and award-winning journalist Maria Shriver.

I will never forget the moment during our first visit with Peggy when I asked who her favorite poet was, making the false assumption that she would offer Robert Frost or Henry Wadsworth Longfellow. Imagine my surprise when, after a moment's contemplation, she replied, "Billy Collins!" Thank you Billy for so generously reading Peggy's poems and thrilling us all with your ringing endorsement!

Geraldine Brooks has the distinction of being the most fabulous reciter of Peggy's words. At an evening salon where we read aloud many of the poems, it was Geraldine's reading that gave us all goose bumps. We also thank her for her insightful notes on this manuscript.

LAURIE TAKING PEGGY'S FIRST SELFIE

Thanks to Maria for her guidance and for loving poetry as much as I do, and to Monina Von Opel for immediately jumping in to produce a proper celebratory Island event for the publication of Poems from the Pond. Thanks to Peter Stray for contributing his editing skills to this project.

Thank you to the Poetry Society of America's Elise Paschen, Alice Quinn, Ruth Kaplan, and Kate Gale for honoring Peggy with your recognition of her work.

A personal thank you to Nancy Aronie who was so moved by Peggy's poems she decided to honor them the best way she could think of – by inviting her friends over to read the poems aloud. Thank you to all the readers that day, including Gerald Blake Storrow, Niki Patton, Fan Olgivie, Fae Kontje-Gibbs, Susan Copen Oken, Kay Goldstein, Doreen Beinart, Valerie Sonnenthal, Paula Lyons, and Arnie Reisman. No one there that magical afternoon left the same as they had come. That was a gift indeed.

Lastly, our deepest thanks go directly to Peggy for trusting us with her precious work. These poems go straight to our hearts. They keep us warm, they keep us company, and they have become lifelong friends. What words can adequately express the gratitude for that?

Laurie David

PHOTO COURTESY OF PEGGY'S PERSONAL COLLECTION

Peggy Freydberg died on March 27, 2015 in her favorite place
surrounded by her favorite people: at home overlooking Stonewall Pond,
embraced by her family and nestled by her cat. A week before,
she saw the final draft of this book and was 'very pleased' that
her poetry was about to be released into the world.

All profits from the sale of this book will go to the
Margaret Howe Freydberg Scholarship Fund.

ISBN 978-0-692-37653-9

52999>